Moments of Being

Deepika

BookLeaf Publishing

India | USA | UK

Made with ❤ on the BookLeaf Publishing Platform

www.bookleafpub.in

www.bookleafpub.com

Dedication

This collection of poems is a labor of love, born from the inspiration and support of those closest to me.

To my parents, who nurtured my heart and mind, I thank you for your unwavering love and guidance. To my husband and daughter, who bring joy and light to my life, I cherish our moments together and appreciate your encouragement. And to my entire family, who have been my foundation, my comfort, and my strength, I acknowledge your role in shaping me into the person I am today.

Thank you for being the melody that fills my heart and soul. This collection is a tribute to our love, laughter, and life's journey together.

Preface

Welcome to my journey of self-discovery, love, and growth. This collection of poems is a reflection of my inner world, where I've navigated the complexities of life, relationships, and my own identity. Through these poems, I invite you to join me on a path of exploration, where I've confronted my fears, celebrated my triumphs, and surrendered to the beauty of the present moment.

From the depths of love and anger to the heights of self-acceptance and inner peace, these poems represent my quest for authenticity, compassion, and connection. May these words resonate with you, inspire you, and remind you that you are not alone on your own journey. May they encourage you to embrace your uniqueness, to radiate love, and to find solace in the beauty of your own heart.

Thank you for holding this space with me.

Acknowledgements

This collection of poems is a tapestry woven with the threads of love and support, and I am profoundly grateful to those who contributed to its creation. To my family, my sanctuary and wellspring of inspiration, your love is the very essence of my words. To my cherished friends, your presence is a constant melody of encouragement. To my fellow poets and writers, your artistry ignites my own creative flame. To my editors and reviewers, your insightful guidance has refined this work. And to every soul who has graced my life, thank you for being a part of my story. This book is a testament to the beautiful power of community, and I am humbled to share it with you.

Radiate love

We radiate what's within our soul
Our energy, a subtle vibe that makes us whole
Positivity, joy, and love we share
Touching hearts, with care

Our presence is a gift, a treasure to behold
A reflection of our heart, a story to be told
People remember us for the joy we bring
The love we share, the laughter we sing

Each of our actions, a brushstroke on the canvas of life
Each of our words, a note that resonates with strife
Our gestures, a language that speaks louder than words
A reflection of our heart, a message that's heard

We reflect on what is within, a mirror to our soul
Our true self, a radiance that makes us whole
We are the creators of our own destiny
Our thoughts, emotions, and actions, a symphony

Let's radiate joys, as it makes the world a better place
A haven of love, where hearts can find their space
Let's spread kindness, compassion, and love everywhere
A ripple effect of positivity, that's beyond compare

We are the change we wish to see, a power to transform
Our lives, a masterpiece, that's yet to be formed
Let's weave a tapestry of love, with every thread
A beautiful work of art, that's born in our hearts forever

I remember people for their bodily gestures, so true
As they speak loudly and clearly, of what lies within
them, anew
Their words, a reflection of their heart, a message that's
clear
A language that speaks louder than words, and brings us
near

To reflect on what is within, a mirror to our soul
Our true self, a radiance that makes us whole
Radiate joys, as it makes the world a better place
A haven of love, where hearts can find their space.

I adore you

In awe, I stand, before those I adore
Elder souls, with hearts that give and more
Their simplicity, a virtue to behold
A lesson to me, in a world that's grown cold

When tasks arise, they step forward with ease
"I'll do it," they say, with a gentle breeze
No fuss, no fanfare, just a willing heart
A quality that sets them apart

Their generosity, a gift to us all
A shelter from life's storms, where we can stand tall
They take the weight, and carry the load
A burden shared, with a heart that's bold

Their presence in my life, a treasure to behold
A guiding light, that shines like gold
Their life teachings, a legacy to share
A heritage of kindness, beyond compare

I'm grateful for these role models in my life
Who show me how to live, with a heart that's rife
With compassion, empathy, and love that's true
A reflection of the beauty, that shines in me and you

In their footsteps, I strive to walk each day
To emulate their kindness, in every single way
To be a source of comfort, a shelter from the storm
A reflection of the love, that they've shown me, and
formed

Here's to these elders, who've touched my heart
A tribute to their kindness, a brand new start
May their example inspire, and guide me on my way
To be a force for good, every single day.

Love n Light

Your greatest responsibility is to yourself, it's true,
Be kind and gentle, and see yourself through.
Let go of discomfort, and don't let it reside,
You are your own caretaker, be your own guide.

Blame, complaints, and negativity will weigh you down,
Block your path, and dim your inner crown.
They'll limit your view, and hold you back from growing,
And weaken your aura, with each negative thought
flowing.

I've learned from my past, from words that hurt and
scarred,
That the harm was mine, and the weight was mine to
mar.
But I sought to cleanse, to purify and renew,
To align with love, faith, and care, and see things anew.

My spirituality guided me, with gentle, loving care,
And helped me find calm, and a new perspective to

share.
I glow with inner light, and step into each new day,
With gratitude, awareness, and a heart that's on its way.

I honor my words, and use them with gentle might,
To uplift and inspire, and shine with love and light.

Memories

Memories, treasures of the heart
Forever cherished, never to depart
Feelings and moments, shared with glee
Love and laughter, forever with me

Gifts and memories, from special souls
Each one a story, that makes me whole
Grateful for the love, they bring to me
Treasured moments, forever in my memory

Heartfelt thanks, for the memories we share
Love and connection, beyond compare
Treasured in my heart, forever to stay
Memories of love, guiding me on my way.

Best moments are etched deep in my heart
They are feelings
No records of any sort
These belong to me and are close to my heart

Gestures

The art of acknowledgment, a subtle, loving deed
A gentle nod, a smile, a response in time, indeed
It takes but a moment, to show we care
A simple gesture, that speaks volumes, beyond compare

A returned smile, a message replied
A presence acknowledged, a support applied
These small acts of kindness, reveal our heart's intent
A reflection of our character, for all to invent

Imagine the ripple effect, of such thoughtful deeds
A wave of love and joy, that spreads with gentle speed
Let's master this art, of acknowledgment true
And become the torchbearers, of love and kindness anew

Small changes can bring, a world of difference wide
Let's choose to be the light, that shines with love inside
For in being the change, we wish to see
We'll find the joy of spreading love n joy being carefree.

Love and Anger

We hide our love, but show our anger bold
A sign of weakness, love's gentle hold
Anger's loud and clear, a popular display
A raised voice, for a fleeting attention and display

But love's a quiet thing, a silent, gentle art
A feeling that's kept hidden, deep within the heart
No need for popularity, when love's true and real
No need to announce, this simple, heartfelt feel

Anger's harsh and loud, a signal to beware
A warning of limits, a message to share
But love's a soft whisper, a gentle, guiding light
A warmth that heals, a hurt that takes flight

Keep it simple, light, and purposeful, we're told
Let go of what's not right, and keep love's light to hold
For in the end, it's not about the anger we show
But about the love we share, and the kindness we grow.

My lessons

We learn and grow from life's ups and downs,
From experiences that test our hearts and crowns.
Discomfort and pain can teach us a lot,
Helping us become stronger, wiser, and more confident
on the spot.

When we're low, we find inner strength to rise,
When we fail, we learn to adapt and open new eyes.
Rejection and ignorance can be tough to face,
But they help us discover our worth and find our own
pace.

Life's experiences, both good and bad, shape us to be,
Stronger, wiser, and more compassionate, wild and free.
Let's embrace life's lessons, and learn from each fall,
And rise again, stronger and wiser, standing tall.

Repeating patterns is thing of the past
Something learnt and not to part
Look ahead and bright

Learn from each fall as you climb.

Embracing Me

I once hid my age, afraid to reveal
But life's secrets unfolded, and I began to heal
I learned to love myself, in every phase
And found solace in my uniqueness, my heart's own
ways

I chased the wind, seeking more and more
But spirituality whispered, 'Look within, and adore'
The beauty in my flaws, the strength in my soul
I began to cherish me, making my heart whole

My weight, my grey hair, my imperfect skin
Once insecurities, now a beauty to win
My husband's words, a balm to my heart
'Your uniqueness is your charm, a work of art'

No pretenses, just a simple me
Living life untethered, joyfully n being carefree
Covid's stillness taught me to look within
And find comfort in my own skin, like a long-forgotten

kin

My struggles, my journey, my story to share
But in embracing myself, I've found a love that's rare
I may not fit your mold, but I'm enough, just as I am
A masterpiece, unfinished, yet uniquely planned

Why conform to expectations? I'm free to be
I'll take care of me, and share my authenticity
Rise each day, and celebrate your unique way
Blow your trumpet loud, and start each day

Be yourself

Be yourself, it's the best fit,
Don't try to be someone else, it's not worth the hit.
Your mannerisms, your style, your voice, it's all you,
Don't copy, don't fake, just be true.

Speak from your heart, let your words flow free,
Don't try to be someone else, it's just not you, see.
Inspiration is key, not imitation, that's the way,
To shine so bright, in your own unique way.

You're one of a kind, a masterpiece, so rare,
Don't try to be someone else, show the world you care.
Being you is timeless, it's the best trend,
So own it, rock it, and let your true self transcend.

Be you, it's the best way to be
Don't copy, just yourself be
Your uniqueness shines so bright
Don't hide it, let it light up the night

Speak your truth, let your voice be heard
Don't fake it, just be wonderful n true
Inspire, don't imitate, that's the key
To being you, lovely and free.

Faith n Flow

A tsunami of thoughts, a stormy sea
Questions, whys, and what-ifs, swirling me
Some I grasp, some slip away
Some clear with time, while others stay

In my highs and lows, they surface and roam
As I delve deeper, new insights come home
Some sharpen my mind, while others make me smile
Some leave me pondering, in a questioning while

But I've learned to see, that these thoughts aren't random
or free
They appear to guide me, to what needs attention from
me
Wisdom lies in placing them right, in their proper place
Some I control, while others, I learn to face

Yet, despite my efforts, I sometimes lose my way
And fall into the rut, night and day
But I've found solace, in letting thoughts flow

Not letting them impact me, as they ebb and go

Time and the universe, will unfold what's meant to be
Why worry now, and waste my energy?
Faith and flow, calm my mind and soul
Higher forces are at work, making me whole.

Two guiding keys

Life's two guiding keys,
Do what's required, with humility,
And don't knock on closed doors, thrice,
Respect boundaries, and let go with ease.

Cultivate peace, tranquility, and growth,
By releasing what's not meant to be,
Trusting the universe's gentle hold,
To bring what's yours, in perfect timing's mould.

Let go of attachment, and move ahead,
Focus on the present, and let the future unfold instead,
Trust that what's meant for you, will find its way,
Have faith in the universe's perfect plan each day.

My Best

A journey of self-discovery I did stride
With healing practices, I did reside
Ho'oponopono, a path I did choose
Mixed results, yet lessons to relearn

Confusion and vulnerability, I did face
Yet, my heart remained open, a sacred space
Despite the challenges, I did try once more
Attracted to , I wanted to explore

But the universe whispered, "Move away"
In dreams and intuition, I heard what to say
Betrayal and lies, the signs did unfold
Yet, I gave another chance, my heart to mould

Blocked on social media, a message I did see
A test of time, patience, and destiny
When I checked again, the truth did reveal
A confirmation of what my heart long back did feel

The universe sent clues, a guiding light
To move away, and end this untidy ...
I'm grateful for the experience, a lesson learned
A closed door, a new path that yearns

To be liberated, peaceful, and free
A joy within, a heart full of glee
I cherish the closure, a new dawn unfolds
A story of growth, of heart and soul

Thank you, universe, for the signs and the test
For helping me grow, and find my best
I'm grateful for the journey, the highs and the lows
A story of self-love, of heart and soul that glows

Perimenopause

A timeless lesson I've held dear,
To do one thing at a time, always clear.
It keeps my focus sharp and bright,
And reminds me to move forward with all my might.

In this phase of life, where mind and body sway,
Peri-menopause brings its own unique day.
When clutter and fog creep in, I remind myself to stay,
Simple, focused, and moving forward, come what may be

Complete this task, before the next begins,
Keep it simple, and let your spirit win.
This mindset etches itself, a guiding light,
To tackle life's challenges, with focus and might.

When confusion and overwhelm start to creep,
I remind myself, one thing at a time, I'll keep.
I complete my tasks with dedication and care,
My goal is completion, not perfection, I gladly share.

I've left perfection far behind, it's no longer my test,
I'm at peace, no competition, no need to stress.
I simply focus on what's at hand,
And trust that all will unfold, in its own perfect plan.

Triggers

Triggers are my barometers, gauging life's turbulent tide,
Pointing to areas within, where my growth and wisdom
reside.
Complaints of hurt and pain may arise,
But those triggers reveal hidden lessons and a chance for
me to realize.

They come and go, moments which test my soul,
Rudeness, ignorance, and hurt, not my heart's goal.
Yet those triggers remind me to look within,
To understand my needs and let love and wisdom win.

Unreasonable and rude, they may seem at first sight,
But triggers teach me such valuable lessons in the
darkest of night.
Now I pay attention to each trigger's call,
And use them as guides to navigate life's wall.

For in their uncomfortable truth lies a hidden gift,
A chance to grow, to learn, and to shift.

Triggers, my teachers, my guides also my friends,
Helping me navigate life's journey rightfully to the very end.

The Fight Within

The battle's not outside, but deep within
A choice to hold on tight or let go and begin
Can I control what I see? Can I calm the storm?
Can I ask others to change, or is it my heart that must
form?

I used to fight, to rearrange and correct
Spending time internalizing, trying to perfect
I'd straighten others mat, align their slippers with care
Tidy others' spaces, offer advice, though unasked to
share

But slowly, I realized it's not my role
To fix others' lives, to take control
Let them be, let things unfold
Don't disturb the balance, let it remain untold

I learned to give only when asked
To respect boundaries, to let them do their task
I found peace in embracing myself and others too

In letting go, in trusting, in seeing as they are , old or
new

Now, I remind myself, it's not my job to do
If others want, they'll ask, they'll see it through
I'll do my part, but theirs is their own
My peace is my responsibility, my heart's throne

I've learned to let go, to not be perturbed
To focus on my work, to trust others will learn
There's a subtle difference between knowing what to do
And respecting others' paths, their journey they know

With awareness, I still make mistakes
But now, I don't dwell, I learn, I grow, I awake
Life's lessons are precious, they guide me along
I'm grateful for the journey, for the growth and all the
songs.

How to Hold Space for the Hurting

Don't dismiss their pain with a careless phrase,
Or judge their heart with a critic's gaze.
Don't assume you know what they're going through,
Or offer empty words that bring no comfort true.

Don't shut your doors or turn away,
For in their darkness, they need your gentle stay.
Don't laugh or scorn, or tell them to be strong,
For in their vulnerability, they need your loving song.

Don't offer clichés that minimize their strife,
Or tell them to "grow up" and end their cries .
Don't gossip or spread rumors that bring them shame,
Or use their trust to fuel your own selfish game.

Instead, be present, and let them feel your heart,
Let them cry, and hold them close, a brand new start.
Help them feel, and heal, and find their inner strength,
And when they're ready, help them learn to love again

again n again.

Be wise, help them lean and trust you too
Knowing not everyone will do this with love so true
Create your awareness, surround yourself with more
love
And, when you are hurting, know that you are sent from
above.

Hold space for the hurting, and be a wonderful soul ,
Remain there till they say now I don't need you
anymore.

It radiates back to me

When I speak words of kindness, they reverberate back
to me,
A gentle echo that resonates, a harmony of love and glee.
Whatever I do, whoever I uplift and praise,
The same radiant energy returns, a warm and fuzzy haze.

I've intentionally praised others with a genuine heart,
Not seeking brownie points or a reciprocal start.
But to bask in the joy, the love that overflows,
To see them glow, to feel their delight, as it grows.

It's pure bliss, a magic that's hard to define,
A therapy that heals, a love that's simply sublime.
Good karma that multiplies, a boomerang of love,
Returning to me, sent from above.

The light I shine on others falls back on me,
A beautiful cycle, a love energy.
It's a feeling that's hard to put into any scene ,
A sense of connection, a love that's unfurled.

I'll keep shining my light, spreading love and kindness
too,
And watch as it returns, a beautiful love that's true.
In the end, it's not just about what we give,
But the love and joy we receive, and in the hearts that
we live.

I love to see ,
When it's looking for me .
Waiting for the glory n radiance
Shine back on me

Happy People

Sometimes those happy hearts are masked n smile so
wide,
Conceal their pain, and spread it like tide .
They judge and criticize, with words that cut and divide,
Feeling joy in others' tears and make misery their life

They fuel the fire of gossip and revel in pain,
Predicting misery and loving the blame.
Loud with hatred, they rejoice in others' strife,
Breaking promises, lying, and manipulating with life.

But happy people create happiness n joy wherever they
roam,
Spreading calm , kindness, and love, making the world a
better home.
Their hearts are full of love, their spirits free and bright,
Radiating warmth and touching hearts with delight.

Happy people are happy, and they spread happiness too,
A contagious joy that touches hearts and sees them

through.
Let's focus on kindness and spreading love and light,
And leave the unhappy hearts to be in their own delight.

Happy people elevate spaces with their being ,
Adding color n sheen as holy beings.
They love life and everyone around ,
I rejoice , value their presence, and hold them tight

Some gaps are a blessing

Gaps are good, they give us space
To breathe, to think, to find our pace
A vacuum to fill, a choice to make
To grow, to learn, for our own sake

In quietness, we find our way
Through boredom, to a brand new day
No noise, no distractions, just the sound
Of our hearts beating, our souls unbound

Sometimes we feel lost, alone and blue
But in those gaps, we find our clue
To rise above, to see and to know
That life's too short, to let moments go

I met a friend, after years apart
A dear one, with a loving heart
We drifted away, without a word
But our feelings remained, forever unheard

We met again, by chance, at the airport gate
I was hesitant, but then I didn't wait
I said hello, and opened my arms wide
And we hugged, with hearts full of pride

Years of silence, melted away
As we connected, in a brand new way
With mature hearts, and minds that had grown
We realized, our gap was a blessing in disguise, all along

I like such people

I like people who are real and true,
Their honesty makes me feel happy and new
Their energy is bright, like a sunny day,
It makes me feel alive, in a happy way

I love their style, which is unique and fun,
Shows me who they are inside out
Their persona is cool, like work of art,
Makes me feel happy and always touches my heart

I'm in awe of their mannerisms ,
Their attitude
How easily they say
It's ok, I'm there, I'll take care

I admire people who lift others high,
Who help them feel good, and say kind words of delight
Their love shines like a light,
It makes me feel warm and feels so light.

I admire their boundaries ,
Also what they have achieved
Such people are so easy going
No burden to people, please

I also like people who are confident and free,
Who are themselves, and happy to be ,
They make me feel light and inspired too,
They show me what it means, to be true.

I always love seeing them ,
Appreciate they are part of my contacts list,
They only believe in giving ,
Move fast as are quick by not being struck up in
anything

My list is long n really long
I love people who are all the above n much more
They silently teach me how to grow and glow
I'm happy I know such good souls.

It does get sorted out

Sometimes, life's tangled threads easily unwind,
Through talk, analysis, and discussion, clarity is defined.
But when confusion reigns, and patience wears thin,
Remember, nature has its way, and answers will unfold
within.

In the waiting, don't force, don't strain,
For in the stillness, clarity will reign.
Through someone, something, a reaction will ignite,
Guiding you forward, through the darkest night.

I've learned to let go, to surrender and wait,
Allowing life's natural flow to create and participate.
People will move, reveal, and provide the way,
Bringing clarity to the questions that plagued my day.

So whenever discomfort strikes, and uncertainty reigns,
Take a step back, breathe, and let life's wisdom lead.
Divert your mind, and simply wait,

For in the unfolding, truth will create its own state.

Missing out

Sometimes, knowing less is more,
Missing out is a gain, and a peaceful shore.
Losing sight of some, brings calm to the mind,
A protection from energy drains, left behind.

Their absence is a blessing, a saving grace,
A therapy that heals, and a peaceful space.
Missing them by a second, saved me from strife,
A comment, judgment, or disrespect, cut like a knife.

Less is more, when peace and calm are key,
Withholding reactions, sets the heart free.
No anger bursts, no mood swings to bear,
Just blissful ignorance, and a peaceful air.

The universe conspired, to bring me this gain,
A cherished bliss, that I'll forever sustain.
Missing out was a blessing, a gift from above,
A reminder that sometimes, less is more, and filled with
love.

A saving grace
All in sight for my might

Laugh it off

Laugh and feel light, a treasure so rare,
An underrated secret, to a life beyond compare.
A simple smile, a stretch of the face,
Unfolds positivity, and a joyful, peaceful space.

This easy exercise, relaxes and sets me free,
Making me feel light, being open and carefree.
It's a magnetic force, that attracts what's right,
Putting me on high, where love and joy take flight.

A flex of the muscles, a sparkle in the eyes,
Gathers positivity, and a heart full of surprise.
It's a reminder to smile and laugh with glee,
Creating ripples of joy, wherever I may be.

I remind myself, to laugh and smile each moment and
day,
To break free from emotions, that might lead astray.
No alcohol or sedatives, to suppress or deviations,
Just the pure joy of laughter, to elevate my soul's

vibrations.

It's simple and doable, this secret to delight,
Try to smile and laugh, and let your spirit take flight.
For in the laughter and joy, we find our peaceful nest,
A treasure so rare, that's always at its best.

Yes You

You shine so bright, with a heart so true,
A pillar of strength, in all you do.
Your energy's contagious, it spreads like a flame,
You're a beacon of hope, with a spirit that's not tamed.

I'm so proud of you, for all that you've achieved,
For your courage, your heart, and your spirit that's
relieved.
You're a shining star, that sparkles with glee,
A treasure to behold, a wonder to see.

May your dreams come true, may your heart be light,
May you shine so bright, like a guiding light.
I love you more than words, can say or express,
You're a blessing, a gift, a treasure to caress.

You deserve all the best, all the love and the light,
You're a precious gem, that shines with delight.
Keep shining your light, keep spreading your love,

You're a blessing to all, sent from above.

A Heartfelt Thank You

Your kindness touches my soul,
In ways that words alone can not unfold.
A helping hand, a gentle deed,
It was a thoughtful gesture that my heart could read.

A lift, a held door, a guiding light,
It is a comforting presence that makes everything right.
A shared number, a sitting friend,
A reassuring nod that never ends.

A warm hug, holding my hand tight ,
Your love and care are forever shining bright .
A message sent, a text, a simple glance,
Speaks volumes of love without a second chance.

Your kindness asks, 'Are you sure you're fine?'
Assurance and care, a love that's truly divine.
I see the beauty in these everyday deeds,
A love that's pure, a heart that truly proceeds.

The words I speak, a heartfelt 'Thank you' so apt and
true,
Simplicity in meaning, yet a depth that shines through.
Purifying my heart, uplifting my soul,
A sense of gratitude that makes me whole.

In these small moments, love shines bright and clear,
A treasure trove of kindness, always near.
No grand gestures needed, just a genuine heart,
A love that's felt, a love that doesn't set us apart.

Thank you one more time
For all that you do
Even more gratitude for that loud n quiet NO
It helped me open up and taught me how to grow !!